Contents

Composer's note

'Trumpet Tune' was written for *The Oxford Book of Wedding Music*. Dedicated to Geoffrey Coffin, for some time assistant organist at York Minster, it was first performed by his successor, John Scott Whiteley, at a wedding in nearby St Wilfrid's church.

'Aria' was penned for Irene Ator and inspired by the von Beckerath organ she played at Fort Wayne United Methodist Church, Indiana. The opening melody and its subsequent appearance in the tenor register reflect two particular stops of this instrument—the sesquialtera and the English horn. This is the instrument whose case is pictured on the cover of this book.

'Saint Wilfrid's Suite' refers to the seventh-century Northumbrian bishop, patron saint of many churches in northern England. For the three-manual Harrison instrument at St Wilfrid's in Harrogate, organist Timothy Gray commissioned an organ mass to be played at the centenary service. Of the five movements, the first is a chorale prelude on Sydney Nicholson's hymn tune *Crucifer*, sung in the opening procession. For Communion, the melody of *Veni Creator* is treated in canon, first at the octave and then the fifth.

'Christmas Canon' is on the tune *Forest Green*, associated in Britain with the text 'O little town of Bethlehem'. It is a reworking of an early handbell score.

Dedicated to a long-standing friend and accomplished organist, Michael Phipps, 'Toccata on *Veni Emmanuel*' was first performed at a recital given by John Scott in York Minster.

ANDREW CARTER
November 2003

4

Trumpet Tune

to Geoffrey and Pam Coffin

Duration: 3′ 20″

This piece also appears in the OUP anthology *The Oxford Book of Wedding Music* (ISBN 0–19–375119–4).

Andrew Carter
Organ Album

MUSIC DEPARTMENT

OXFORD
UNIVERSITY PRESS

Great Clarendon Street, Oxford OX2 6DP, England
198 Madison Avenue, New York, NY10016, USA

Oxford University Press is a department of the University of Oxford.
It furthers the University's aim of excellence in research, scholarship,
and education by publishing worldwide

First published 2004

3 5 7 9 10 8 6 4 2

ISBN 0-19-375322-7

Music and text origination by
Enigma Engraving Ltd., East Sussex
Printed in Great Britain on acid-free paper by
Caligraving Limited, Thetford, Norfolk

poco rit.   a tempo

allarg.   a tempo

Gt. + Sw. *ff*

+ reed

Full + Tpt.

Bishopthorpe, York, December 1986

for Irene S. Ator and the von Beckerath organ
of First Wayne Street United Methodist Church, Fort Wayne, Indiana

Aria

Duration: 3′ 45″

8', 4' Fl. + Sesq.

Bishopthorpe, York, spring 1995

for Timothy Gray.
Commissioned for the Centenary of St Wilfrid's Church, Harrogate in 2002

Saint Wilfrid's Suite

1. Procession

Chorale prelude on *Crucifer*

Duration: 13' 30"

First performed by Timothy Gray at the Parish Mass on Sunday 6th October 2002 on the three manual Harrison organ.

8' + 4' Reeds *mf*

14

2. Gospel Fanfare

3. Offertory

4. Veni Creator Spiritus
(for Communion)

20

5. Finale

Bishopthorpe, York, August 2002

A Christmas Canon on *Forest Green*

English folk melody

Melody collected and adapted by Ralph Vaughan Williams (1872–1958); used by permission of Oxford University Press.

Duration: 2′ 20″

Bishopthorpe, York, spring 1995

for Michael Phipps, with admiration

Toccata on *Veni Emmanuel*

15th-century French melody

Duration: 4' 30"

This piece also appears in the OUP anthology *The Oxford Book of Christmas Organ Music* (ISBN 0–19–375124–0).

Bishopthorpe, York, February 1995